Wisdom Tales in an imprint of World Wisdom, Inc.

Most recent printing indicated by last digit below:

10 9 8 7 6 5 4 3 2

Library of Congress Cataloging-in-Publication Data

Names: Demi, author.
Title: Hildegard of Bingen : scientist, composer, healer, and saint / by Demi.
Description: Bloomington : Wisdom Tales, 2019. |
Identifiers: LCCN 2018042182 (print) | LCCN 2018052404 (ebook) | ISBN
9781937786786 (epub) | ISBN 9781937786779 (casebound : alk. paper)
Subjects: LCSH: Hildegard, Saint, 1098-1179--Juvenile literature. | Christian
women saints--Germany--Biography--Juvenile literature.
Classification: LCC BX4700.H5 (ebook) | LCC BX4700.H5 D455 2019 (print) | DDC
282.092 [B] --dc23
LC record available at https://url.emailprotection.link/?aQIGj4lOvUgMGIEdjJ2U_yMP1Pz2yg1JhzhqEBlgPHic~

Printed in China on acid-free paper.

For information address Wisdom Tales,
P.O. Box 2682, Bloomington, Indiana, 47402-2682
www.wisdomtalespress.com

Hildegard of Bingen

Scientist, Composer, Healer & Saint

Demi

Once upon a time in 1098 AD, in Mainz, Germany,
a little girl was born named Hildegard.

She was a very special girl, because when she shut her eyes, she saw lights, and inside those lights were pictures of Heaven.

When she was three years old her inside lights became so dazzling and bright, that they would make her whole body tremble and shake.

Her lights told her many things. If she looked at a mother cow, she could tell the color of its calf before it was born. She could also predict the future.

But after seeing so many things with her lights, she got terrible headaches. Her parents decided to send her to the Benedictine Cloister of Mount St. Disibod. This monastery was on a beautiful mountain illuminated by the sun. It was a place where people who saw God could go and pray.

Hildegard learned reading, music, singing, Biblical history, prayer, spinning, and work. She was so musical that she could hear the singing of an entire prayer service just once and perform it.

She said, "There is the music of Heaven in all things and we have just forgotten how to hear it until we sing it!"

When Hildegard was eighteen, she became a nun and took the Benedictine habit. She was so wise and so kind that when she was older, Hildegard was elected Abbess of the cloister.

But now when Hildegard shut her eyes, her secret lights were so blinding and her headaches so great that she could hardly bear it any longer.

Then, suddenly, she heard a voice that said:

"This is the voice of God....
When you see a great light inside you,
that too is the light of God....
You must let other people see what you see.
You must let your inside lights shine out."

And so Hildegard began to tell what she saw in her secret land of lights to a nun and monk who wrote it down in a book called *Know the Ways of God*. Hildegard's secret lights showed how to live for God and enter His heavenly city. As Hildegard wrote down what she saw, her headaches also went away. But she wondered if she should tell everything she saw in her secret land of lights.

She thought, "I am just a poor, little woman. I am just a feather on the breath of God."

The greatest monk of the time, Bernard of Clairvaux, told her to continue sharing her secret lights, and so did Pope Eugenius III.

W hen Hildegard was fifty-three, she finished her book *Know the Ways of God* and became famous. Now everyone wanted to see her at St. Disibod Cloister, but it wasn't big enough. Hildegard prayed and received heavenly guidance to move her nuns to Rupertsberg near the town of Bingen.

And so she became known as
Hildegard of Bingen.

At age sixty-five, Hildegard finished her second work, *The Book of Life's Merits*, showing how man can rise to Heaven by overcoming his faults. Hildegard and her nuns could cure many people, because she had studied the ways of Heaven and earth. She now finished her third book, *Physica* (on natural history), and a fourth book, *Causes and Cures* (a scientific and medical encyclopedia). Her fifth book, *The Book of Divine Works*, was on the activity of God that came from five of her secret lights.

Hildegard wrote five more books, and one of them was a cookbook!

So great was Hildegard's secret land of lights, so energetic, so brilliant, and so full of ideas, that Hildegard was able to compose seventy-seven symphonic songs and an operatic morality play. She also wrote hundreds of letters all over the world to emperors, popes, bishops, archbishops, nuns, and nobility. And she invented an alphabet and created a whole new language!

In her sixties and seventies Hildegard made many preaching, teaching, healing, and prophesying tours throughout Germany, and organized and reformed many monasteries.

At the age of eighty-one, Hildegard died on September 17, 1179. She has been considered a saint by Catholics and many Protestants, who celebrate her life and everything she gave to the world from her secret land of heavenly lights.

Appendix

✠   Hildegard's collection of music and poetry, *Symphonia Armonie Celestium Revelationum* ("The Symphony of the Harmony of the Heavenly Revelations"), comprises as many as seventy-seven songs, making her the most prolific composer of early music in Europe.

✠   Hildegard's operatic music drama, *Ordo Virtutum* ("Play of the Virtues"), perhaps the very first of its kind, is a morality play about the struggle between the seventeen virtues and the devil over the destiny of a female soul.

✠   Hildegard's pioneering scientific work in her book *Physica* ("Natural History") formed the basis for the study of natural history in Germany.

✠   Hildegard became renowned as a "spiritual healer" through her medical book *Causae et Curae* ("Causes and Cures"). In exploring the holistic relationship between the human body and the natural world, Hildegard provided cures for a range of human diseases through the use of tinctures, medicinal herbs, and precious stones.

✠   Hildegard invented a new language called the *Lingua Ignota* or "unknown language." While it is not known for what purpose it was constructed, some speculate that it was a "secret" or "mystical" language used by the nuns at Hildegard's monastery.

✠ Hildegard was the author of a cookbook advocating nutritional "foods of joy" that feed both the body and mind. For a wholesome breakfast, Hildegard recommended a warm meal of toasted spelt bread, fennel tea, and roasted spelt porridge with dried fruits.

✠ Hildegard was formally declared a saint by the Catholic Church on May 10, 2012. In fact, for several centuries already she had been referred to as a saint within the Catholic and Anglican churches, both of whom have continued to celebrate her liturgical feast day on September 17.

✠ Hildegard was declared a Doctor of the Catholic Church on October 7, 2012, placing her in the company of eminent Christian theologians such as Saint Augustine and Saint Thomas Aquinas.

✠ Hildegard's parish and pilgrimage church in Bingen, Germany, houses her holy relics. Her earliest biographers, Gottfried and Theodoric, report that many miracles occurred at her tomb soon after her passing.